AN INNER TRUTH

by
Temi Díaz

illustrations
Jose Navarro

DEDICATION

For Ms. Garcia, thank you for showing your inner light to everyone around you!

This is the story of a young girl called Rachel.
She's creative, she's smart, very friendly and playful.

Mom drove her to school on the first day,
they smiled and they laughed as they drove away.

Rachel couldn't express all the joy in her heart,
the first day of school was an exciting new start.

While Mom got her ready to start the new day,

RACHEL IMAGINED ALL THE FUN COMING HER WAY.

As they walked through the schoolyard, before saying goodbye, Mom stopped to give Rachel a few words of advice.

"Before choosing your new seat take a good look around, making friends is not easy when you're the new kid in town."

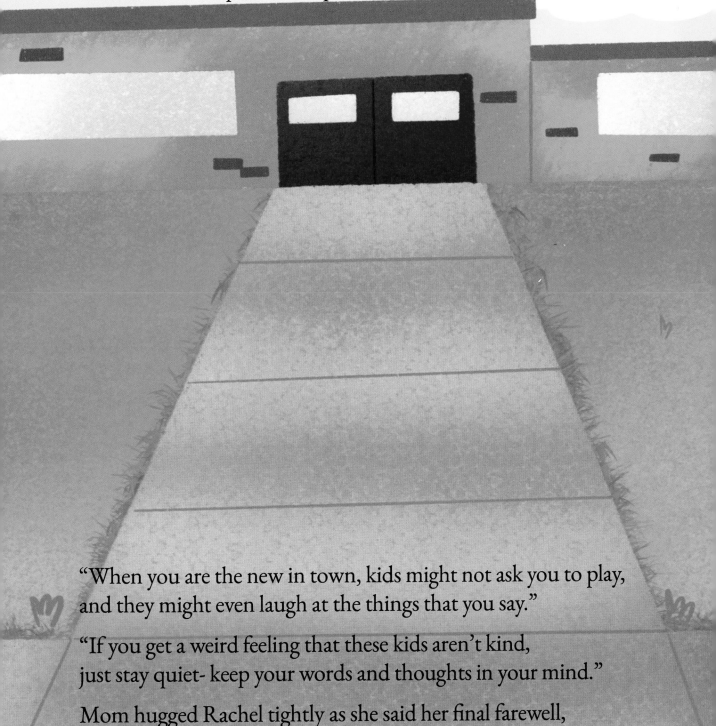

Rachel paused to understand what Mom had just said,
she needed some answers to questions in her head.

"Why wouldn't they be friendly?" Rachel replied.
Mom then explained deeper what she had just advised:

"When you are the new in town, kids might not ask you to play,
and they might even laugh at the things that you say."

"If you get a weird feeling that these kids aren't kind,
just stay quiet- keep your words and thoughts in your mind."

Mom hugged Rachel tightly as she said her final farewell,
and they both hoped that the first day of school would be swell.

She walked towards the classroom with excitement and a big smile,

but as she was approaching the class she paused for a little while.

A sneaky little voice whispered into her head,
it repeated exactly what Mom had just said:

When she walked in the room her smile turned to a frown,
the voice in her head simply would not quiet down.

The teacher noticed Rachel's fears right away,
and quickly came up with the right thing to say.

So, with empathy she walked towards Rachel and said:
"You must be Rachel" who gently nodded her head.

"Children, meet Rachel, she's the new student joining our class today!"
"Hello Rachel!" all the kids said, giving her a warm welcome on the very first day.

Rachel spotted a desk, the perfect spot to sit,
but then the little voice said, "What if this one's NOT IT?"

"You can sit here, there's a desk next to me!"
Said a boy called Andy, who seemed pretty friendly.

Rachel took a step but then froze, she just wasn't sure what to do-
she looked at all the kids faces, frantically searching for a clue.

"If you get a weird feeling that these kids aren't kind,
just stay quiet- keep your words and thoughts in your mind."

Rachel suddenly felt her body turn to a giant gray cloud,
as the fears in her mind were becoming quite loud.

The gray cloud was spreading all through her body
it made her feel invisible, like she was nobody.

The cloud even blurred her entire vision,
hiding her true self, her inner intuition.

"Rachel come play with us!"

all of the kids said.

But her imagination heard,

"They just want to laugh at me"

instead.

And just like that, the first day of school came to an end,
Rachel truly believed that no one wanted to be her friend.

After school Rachel ran to Mom and cried out:
"Everything you told me was true, there's no doubt!"

"Don't worry," Mom said, as she hugged her real tight,
"I'll go talk to your teacher and make sure everything's alright."

Mom met with the teacher, she had so much to say,
and she wanted to hear all about Rachel's first day.

"Rachel came home crying because kids were not friendly.
She felt ashamed, she felt sad and she felt very lonely."

"I'm not surprised at all because it also happened to me.
That's why I warned her just how mean kids could be."

The teacher realized the things that Mom feared,
came from wounds of her childhood that had never
disappeared.

"Your advice to Rachel came from old scars of your own, creating thoughts in her mind that made her feel scared and alone."

"If Rachel shows her own inner light, she will never go wrong, she will meet lots of friends and will always belong."

Mom finally understood what the teacher had said.
She would help Rachel find her guiding light instead.

It was time to show Rachel the strength from within,
that lies deep in our hearts if we only give in.

Sometime pains of the past carry sadness and sorrow,
and we must always look ahead for a better tomorrow.

"I made a big mistake when I gave that advice,
you see, I knew some kids at school who were not very nice."

"You have so many wonderful qualities inside,
so there is no need for you to ever hide."

"By focusing only on the things that COULD go wrong,
I didn't give you confidence to feel that you WOULD belong."

Rachel listened carefully and her mind became clear,
she realized that she really had nothing at all to fear.

"If I show my inner light by being myself, I can never go wrong,
I will meet lots of friends and I will always belong."

The grey clouds completely disappeared,
as Rachel's inner light began to appear.

Mom finally let go of her dark clouds from the past,
allowing her inner light to shine brightly at last.

The next day at school Rachel found the PERFECT spot,
"Sitting close to Andy would be a great choice!" she thought.

"Hello Andy, my name is Rachel!" she said very joyful and playful.

Rachel learned about her own Inner Truth that day,
realizing that by being herself everything would turn out okay.

It's the light that shines bright and glistens,
and it speaks to us only when we choose to listen.

When we smile and show kindness, we glow and we shimmer,
So that sadness or fear won't let us to get dimmer.

Try to follow your senses with an open heart and open mind,
leaving negative thoughts and dark, gray clouds to hover behind.

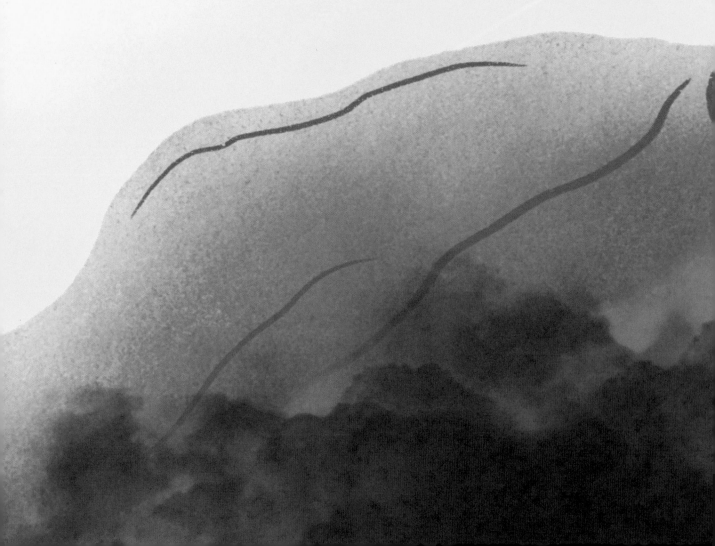

"Be true to yourself, and don't let anyone take the light that you have inside. You are everything you need and if you know this, I promise everything will be alright"

- Temi Diaz

Made in the USA
Middletown, DE
13 October 2020